Collieries of the Sirhowy Valley

by Rayner Rosser

**This book is dedicated
to the Miners of the
Sirhowy Valley
1750 to 1989**

Old Bakehouse Publications

© Rayner Rosser

First published in March 1996

All rights reserved

The right of Rayner Rosser to be identified
as author of this work has been asserted in
accordance with sections 77 and 78 of the
Copyright Designs and Patents Act 1988.

ISBN 1 874538 01 8

Published in the U.K. by
Old Bakehouse Publications
Church Street,
Abertillery, Gwent NP3 1EA
Telephone: 01495 212600   Fax: 01495 216222

Made and printed in the UK
by J.R. Davies (Printers) Ltd.

FOREWORD

Remembering our roots is important - the more so in today's world where consumption is king and it seems nothing is meant to last very long.

My mother never tired of reminding us of these roots with the phrase: 'It is not who you become that matters most, but rather remembering where you come from'.

Rayner Rosser has done an admirable job of reminding us of our roots in this publication about the Sirhowy Valley.

The development of the valley is traced out for us in words and pictures in such a way that the reader cannot fail to identify with it.

As the author herself points out, in such a work it is difficult to know where to begin. I am personally glad she chose to write about our most recent history.

I say this because I believe it is most the interesting and relevant period for study as we go into the new millennium. We need to take stock of the past couple of hundred years or so in order to build a better future.

Our history in these valleys is not that of kings and queens and great lords, but rather of a people moulded and shaped by the industrial revolution.

A revolution which, despite its black side, set working people on the path to economic and political freedom, greater self-esteem and a belief in themselves.

I hope you enjoy this book and get as much pleasure and knowledge out of it as I have done.

Don Touhig MP
February 1996

HOUSE OF COMMONS
LONDON SW1A 0AA

INTRODUCTION

Writing a book about a specific place seems simple enough, places are easy to define, they are usually drawn on a map, photographed and described by many people. The 'where to write about' is not difficult, especially if, like the Sirhowy Valley, it is a fascinating place of enormous variation. The book covers the length of the Valley, from the source of the Sirhowy River, in north Tredegar, travelling south to Risca, ignoring local authority boundaries.

The difficult part, for this author at least, is 'when to begin', and that took a great deal of thinking about. Other authors will have dealt with the evolution of this planet, the pre-history before mankind and the early days of civilisation, when a few hardy people inhabited the hilltops above the Sirhowy River and only took the dangerous climb down through the thick forests that covered the steep hillsides to hunt for food.

I took a leap through the centuries and decided to cover more recent history, to give a very brief profile of the place and the people as it was over the past two hundred years or so. This is not a technical learned history of the Sirhowy, it is intended as an outline study of the evolution of what was a mining community, a reminder of the past. It is a tribute to the colliers who created wealth, mainly for others, and the families who supported them. This story could be repeated throughout the mining communities in the world, it is largely unsung and often under recognised. Now there are no mines in the Sirhowy Valley, it is, once more, a green and lovely place, facing the new challenges of the technological revolution.

The Valley has always changed with the times, but the changes that took place over the period recorded in this book have been most remarkable. It is a different age, but on the map it is the same valley.

Rayner Rosser,

March, 1996

THE EBBW CATCHMENT

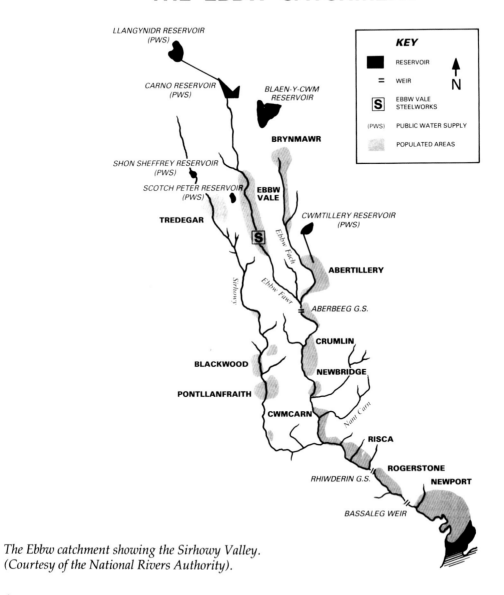

The Ebbw catchment showing the Sirhowy Valley.
(Courtesy of the National Rivers Authority).

CHAPTER ONE

The profile of the communities of the Sirhowy Valley must begin with a brief description of the place. It was the geography and the geology that attracted people to it, a place that was plundered to fuel the Industrial Revolution, that created wealth for some and disaster for others. It is a place of history, where change has been a constant creative and destructive force over the past centuries, and where the population has always needed to adapt to suit a new way of life.

The Sirhowy Valley in South Wales lies between the towns of Tredegar in the north and Newport, on the Severn Estuary, in the south, about two thirds of the town of Tredegar is in the Sirhowy Valley. The Sirhowy River rises from a spring near the Shon Sheffrey Reservoir, north of Tredegar, on the mountain of Trefil Ddu in North West Gwent, about 500 metres above sea level. It flows through a steep and once thickly wooded valley for 32.6 kilometres, until it joins the River Ebbw Fawr at Risca. The Sirhowy is a major tributary of the River Ebbw, which carries water from its source at Mynydd Llangynidr, to the Severn Estuary at the mouth of the River Usk.

The land was called Uwchlaw y Coed in many ancient documents, (meaning 'the land above the woods'). It stretched along the western side of the river from Nantybwch to Argoed. The place called Glynne (meaning a glen) Sirhowy was the valley, which was part of the ancient lordship of Gwynllwg. The hills to the south were thickly wooded, as many place names such as Coed Cae and Coed Cynghordy indicate. The Sirhowy River rushed through the gorge-like slopes of the banks in a clear and shining torrent. Brown and rainbow trout would have been plentiful, as were sticklebacks, minnows, flounders and eels. Otters thrived on the abundance, and built their holts on the banks. The forests were full of animals and birds.

Prior to industrialisation, there were several homesteads in the area which were self-supporting mainly through agriculture. Usually thatched-roof houses of wood and locally quarried stone, they were built by the owners who farmed their own land or helped out on other farms. There was sufficient grain produced to keep a few mills busy, the wool from the local sheep was spun and sent to market in Caerphilly across rough tracks over the hills.

On Manmoel Mountain, in a hollow above the forest, the hamlet of Manmoel had long been a place of local importance, it is believed to have its origins in the twelfth century. Further along the valley, to the south, in the hamlet of Mynyddislwyn, the burial mound of Twyn Tudor indicates a very ancient dwelling place. The name Bedwellty, once the parish name, derives from Bod-wellte, the dwelling of Wellte, a saint or patriarch of ancient times.

The name Sirhowy has at different times had several renditions, including Sirhywi, Sirhowey, Sirowi, Sroway and Sirowy. The origin of the name has also been the subject of intense debate over the years. Eiddil Gwent, the first historian of the area, was of the opinion that the word derived from Siriol Gwy, 'siriol' meaning pleasant or charming, and 'gwy' being the old Welsh word for water, thus the names 'Pleasant Water'. Another clue to its meaning might be the definition in Hughes Welsh Dictionary (1861) which shows 'Sor' to mean angry or sullen, the 'wy' being derived from the original 'gwy' meaning water, indicating this was Angry Water.

The medieval church at Mynyddislwyn - dedicated to St. Tudor.

Other theories, based on stories about battles on the Trefil mountain between the Welsh soldiers and the Normans, have also been debated over the years. The legend is that the exhausted Welsh soldiers were camped for the night near the source of the river, when reports came in that the Normans were nearby and likely to attack in the morning. The Welsh leader rallied his men and asked them *'Who is ready to stand and fight once more?'* His soldiers replied, as one, *'Syr wy 'i'* meaning *'I am, Sir'*. The Welsh won the battle, and the general commemorated the victory by naming the place Syr-wy-'i after their spirited response. An alternative version of the same story gives the name of the general as Sir Howell, known as Sir Howy, who named the river after himself. Whatever the truth is, there is evidence that battle did take place on Trefil Ddu and the name Sirhowy has been related to the river in various forms and spelling for many centuries.

Archdeacon Coxe travelled in the area in 1799. He describes it in his 'Historical Tour of Monmouthshire':

'A lane winds its way down the steep sides of a rugged declivity to the banks of the Sorwy, where a bold stone bridge is thrown over a rocky channel. The view from the bridge is particularly wild; the glen, diminished to a hollow between lofty eminences covered with forests, is wholly occupied by the impetuous torrent.'

The Archdeacon also refers to the Romans who built the Roman Road, Ffordd y Rufeneig across Dukestown from the top of Sirhowy, over Bryn Bach to Rhymney and then to Penydarren. Sarn

8

Hir is the old road leading from Cefn Golau to Bedwellty Church, the original and at one time, the only road leading out of the Glyn to the south. This Roman road was also referred to by the Archdeacon, the word 'Sarn' means a road used by the Romans.

The Romans had also discovered and exploited the mineral wealth of the valley; they had mined ironstone north of Tredegar, and numerous Roman limeworkings and limekilns have been found at Trefil.

The early history of the Sirhowy is that of a place that was home to farmers, usually a place of peace, but sometimes in contrast, a place of battle. It changed little until the beginning of the Industrial Revolution in the eighteenth century.

The geology over the area consists of grits, sandstone and shales which make up the Pennant rock series along with coal measures. To the north, iron ore was discovered in abundant quantities at Nantybwch and Bryn Oer in the eighteenth century, and was smelted in various small furnaces, using charcoal fuel from the nearby woods. The hills around the hamlet of Trefil were rich in

St. Sannan's Church, Bedwellty with its 14th century bell tower.

carboniferous limestone, a much needed commodity for use as a flux, as well as for agriculture and for mixing with mortar.

In the eighteenth century the mill at Nant Melyn, at Dukestown, also had a limekiln. This mill, Mill Farm at Heathfield and the mill at Gelligroes had water wheels driven by the river. Other water powered mills were built in the Valley during the seventeenth and eighteenth centuries.

Oliver Jones records, in his book 'The Early Days of Sirhowy and Tredegar':

'A strip of land, twenty miles long and about two miles wide, stretching from Hirwaun in Glamorganshire to Blaenavon in Monmouthshire, was known to possess all the essentials of good ironmaking and there, the craft of iron smelting spread rapidly. Halfway along the strip, lay the head of the Sirhowy Valley where furnacing began quite early. Here too, the great ironworks of Sirhowy and Tredegar came into existence.'

A small furnace called Pont Gwaith Yr Haearn was used for smelting iron ore on the banks of the Sirhowy a few miles south of the present town of Tredegar in 1738. An even earlier furnace is recorded in a document in the Public Record Office, which describes a Bedwellty furnace working in the Sirhowy Valley in 1597.

The small furnaces, the forerunners to the great ironworks, were mainly established during the eighteenth century and produced a variety of agricultural implements, tools, and domestic utensils such as cooking pots and kettles, which were much in demand. Ironstone was found very easily, being very thinly covered by soil in beds about thirty centimetres deep, surrounded by rock and shale which had to be dug away and removed. When such digging was difficult, adjacent brooks or ponds would be dammed, and when the water was released it would scour off the unwanted material.

The collected ironstone was taken to the small furnaces nearby, where it was smelted down at first using charcoal for fuel. There was a national shortage of wood for charcoal at this time, as so many thousands of acres of trees had been cut down for building houses and ships, as well as for fuel. The need for an alternative was essential, and as coal introduced impurities to the metal, this was not at first considered to be the solution to the problem.

In 1709 Abraham Darby of Coalbrookdale in Shropshire successfully used coke, made from coal, to smelt iron. The South Wales furnace owners realised the potential of this discovery and also turned to this fuel. Coal was converted to coke to remove the sulphur, it then also gave more heat which meant that more iron could be smelted at the same time.

The ample coal that lay near to the surface in the same area as the ironstone was gathered for use, from coal 'levels' or 'drifts'. South Wales coal was found to be ideal for smelting iron, and at the beginning of the Industrial Revolution the main customer for coal was the iron industry.

The earliest reference to the use of coal in Wales (at Neath) was in 1248, but the coal mining industry developed in that area hundreds of years later, in the seventeenth century. In the following century the growth of the iron industry brought about the demand for coal in other areas of South Wales.

Coal was first worked on the surface by the miner digging a shallow tunnel or 'adit', and loading the coal into baskets made of interwoven twigs. This was removed by a coal bearer, often a woman or older child, crawling along the stony floor pushing or dragging the basket in complete darkness to the opening. 'Adits' were also used to drain water from the workings. There were several small coal levels which were working in the Sirhowy Valley before the end of the eighteenth century.

At the same time, the Rhondda, Cynon and Taff Valleys, and other areas of Monmouthshire adjacent to the Sirhowy Valley were also expanding to meet the needs of the new industries. The population explosion in the parish of Bedwellty, which at the time of the first census in 1801 included Rhymney, Tredegar and part of Ebbw Vale had 619 inhabitants; in the 1811 census it had more than trebled to 2,200. In 1861 the figure was 9,383, and thirty years later in 1891 the census showed 17,341.

No-one who saw the wisps of smoke rising through the trees above the valley floor in the early years of the eighteenth century, could have thought that the crude furnaces that caused them were the forerunners of a great industry. The idyllic Sirhowy Valley was about to change for ever.

An exceptionally early and rare photograph of the Tredegar Ironworks locomotive 'St. David' pictured in the year 1854 with Thomas Ellis on the footplate with the driver.

CHAPTER TWO

The closing days of the eighteenth century saw the continuation of the massive changes that had already started to alter the face of the Sirhowy. The tiny original population began to be aware of more strangers in their midst, including many odd people who could not speak Welsh, who knew nothing about local ways. They were mostly young and hardworking, digging all day for ironstone, building small furnaces, leasing land from the farmers for their houses and buying whatever food the locality could supply.

In a very short time it became apparent that more vegetables, grain and meat would be needed to supply these needs if the incomers were to stay. The farming community, which had always had a fairly relaxed way of life, began to find that they were kept busy.

Thomas Price, one of the founders of the Dowlais Ironworks at Merthyr, responding to the increased need for iron, leased several areas in the Bryn Oer and other nearby districts to ensure supplies of iron, coal and also limestone. The mineral resources of the Sirhowy 'mineral belt' were already much in demand.

In 1778 four Englishmen leased some land at Sirhowy from Charles Henry Burgh of the Abercarn Estate to build an ironworks. They also leased some nearby land from Sir Charles Morgan, who owned the Tredegar Estate in Newport. The ironworks, which was completed in 1780, initially produced three tons of pig iron a week, but despite this initial success, the company failed in 1794. The Revd. Matthew Monkhouse and Richard Fothergill took over the lease, and by 1797 had built a new furnace.

With their new partner Samuel Homfray of the Pen-y-darren Ironworks, who was the son-in-law of Sir Charles Morgan, they set up the Tredegar Ironworks on land leased from Sir Charles. They chose the name Tredegar in honour of Sir Charles, whose ancestral title was Lord Tredegar. The town which grew up around the works acquired the same name.

At the time, there were several small furnaces working in the area, on what had been agricultural land, so the erection of the new furnaces by the company in 1800 must have caused a certain amount of disquiet. The new owners employed more people and provided housing for their workers. The new company, also formed in 1800, as the Tredegar Iron Company, had a major impact on the area which was to bring about profound and lasting change.

The woodlands began to ring with the sound of axe and saw as trees were felled to build houses, furniture and carts. For the first time for hundreds of years, many acres of soil were touched by the sun instead of being under a canopy of leaves.

The river too, was changing, the fast flowing mountain river was receiving all the debris from the digging along the banks, some of which was washed along to the coast at Newport, where women were later to gather river-washed coal to sell for a living.

Other than lanes and paths through the woods and across the fields, there were no proper roads in the area. Cinders from the furnaces were used to construct the first road from Sirhowy to the southern part of Tredegar, this was completed in 1811 and the Abergavenny road was

A 1921 map showing the Sirhowy Valley.

commenced. Now workers and materials had easier access to Tredegar, and the goods that were manufactured could be carried to more distant markets.

During this period, from 1750 and over the next one hundred and fifty years, the communities of Georgetown, Sirhowy, Dukestown and Nantybwch developed, as did the central Tredegar town area. The hamlet of Trefil, near to the source of limestone, grew into a village. Limestone was extracted and conveyed by mule to farmers many miles away.

Coal levels at Penmarc, Bryn Bach, Nantybwch and Tarfarnau Bach attracted large numbers of workers, not only from South Wales, but from the West Country and the Midlands.

To keep pace with the growing needs of the furnaces, pits were sunk to mine coal, the Duke's Pit in 1806, being named for the Duke of Beaufort, the owner of the land. This is one of two claimants for the title of the first deep pit in Wales, the other being the Pwll Mawr Pit at Neath, which was sunk at the same time. The site of Duke's Pit is now the Rhoslan Housing Estate in Tredegar.

The increasing market for iron products required more men to produce the ironstone, man the furnaces and fashion the iron. Men, women and children were all employed in this heavy, dangerous work. Most of them were totally unskilled at the jobs they had to do, having been used to working on their farms with their crops and animals. During this time, however, they poured from all over the surrounding areas, to the equivalent of the 'Gold Rush'. Houses were hurriedly built and Tredegar came into being as a town.

The village of Coed Duon (Black Wood) consisted of no more than a few farms and cottages for farm workers at the turn of the century. The village was dominated by four hills, all over 800ft (244 metres), to the northeast at Penmaen and Oakdale, to the northwest at Penllwyn, to the southeast at Mynydd Islwyn and Mynydd Llan and to the southwest Mynydd-y-Grug. The only feasable place for the village to develop was along the valley floor.

The need for efficient routes to and from the now industrial town of Tredegar became obvious to the Tredegar Iron Company. The horses and mules could not manage to haul all the iron and coal that was being exported from the Valley, and the Monmouthshire Canal which opened in 1798, was not the promised solution to the problem as it suffered from a water shortage during the summer and was often unnavigable. Tramroads were considered to be a cheaper and more reliable prospect.

In 1805 the Sirhowy Tramroad was completed, to provide access to and from Newport. More coal than was needed locally was being mined in the new small pits, but there was a ready market at the coast. The Sirhowy Tramroad Company, owned by Samuel Homfray and his partners, had taken the advice of Benjamin Outram, one of the foremost consulting engineers of the day. The Monmouthshire Railway and Canal Company had commissioned him to suggest the best way to carry freight from Tredegar to join the Canal Company's tramroad at Risca.

The Sirhowy Tramroad from Tredegar to Newport was a single track, available to anyone who wanted to haul their freight using their own motive power and wagons. They paid three pence per ton per mile and joined the tramroad at various turnpikes along the route. From Risca, the line was double track and crossed a viaduct span of 32 arches at a height of 48ft (15.75 metres). This track took the trams to the Canal terminus at Llanarth Street, Newport.

The trams were hauled in trains of about 15 by teams of five or six horses, which took all day to travel from Tredegar to Newport. The point where the trams went over to the Canal Company's track, was nine miles from Newport and has since then been called Nine Mile Point. Horses were changed at Blackwood and at Nine Mile Point. A flat cart called a 'Gambo' or 'Dandy Cart' was attached to the rear of the train, so the exhausted horses could ride in turn as passengers for part of the journey.

Records show that by 1806 coal was being transported from a colliery at Gelligroes, to Newport, along the Sirhowy tramroad in horse drawn wagons. It was not an easy ride for man or beast, as the trams had no buffers or brakes, and the inclines were steep. Accidents were common, but despite all the difficulties tons of coal and other goods were conveyed regularly along the tramway.

In 1829 Sir Samuel Homfray, of the Tredegar Iron Company, took part in an experiment on the tramroad, by riding from Tredegar to Newport on a coach drawn by a steam engine 'Britannia', known locally as 'Puffing Billy'. The journey took all day, as the rails broke under the weight and at Bassaleg the funnel of the engine hit the branch of a tree, and Sir Samuel and his party had to continue their journey on foot. 'Britannia' was repaired the next day however, and went on to prove the value of steam locomotives by hauling 50 or 60 tons of coal a day at a reduced cost of 35 per cent.

The journeys were not trouble free, however, as the speed limit imposed by law at this time was ten miles an hour. Another problem was the temptation of the many inns and public houses that had been built along the tramroad, at which the drivers and firemen stopped for occasional refreshment. It was on one such occasion that the boiler blew up, whilst the crew were in 'The George' at Blackwood.

A branch of the Sirhowy Tramroad was also opened to Gellihaf, through the village of Bryn. This brought about the sinking of the Bryn Colliery and opened up yet another area to exploit the mineral wealth. The coal was carried along the Branch to Tredegar Junction, where it joined the Sirhowy Tramroad, and then was carried to Newport.

Along the line of the Sirhowy Tramroad, around the village of Coed Duon, the town which sprang up became the township of Blackwood. The tramroad ran through the area which is now the High Street. At first, like the town of Tredegar, it was no more than a shanty town, with crude huts for the workers, who poured in from other areas of Wales, from the English Midlands and the West Country, in search of work and opportunity.

Blackwood grew quickly as an industrial area. The Rock Foundry was developed in 1823, coal levels were being opened, timber was being felled and stone was being quarried. Around these industries and the ever busy tramroad, Blackwood evolved.

There was an urgent need for blacksmiths, farriers, lumberjacks, carpenters, masons, and perhaps most of all, willing labourers able to turn their hands to anything as long as they were fed and housed. They poured in by the hundred, men, women and children. All they had in common was their poverty and their determination to make a living in this new, strange land.

They lived in appalling squalor in these new townships, living usually in hovels, with no sanitation, water being carried from nearby springs or wells, or even the river. There were no facilities for medical care, and no form of local government to organise services. They took whatever work they could find, irrespective of their age or gender, and there must have been many who thought they had left rural poverty behind and who now found themselves in worse conditions.

The old cemetery at Cefn Golau in Tredegar, holds the graves of many of the victims of the cholera epidemics of 1831 and 1849, when entire families were wiped out by disease.

The eerie and isolated 19th century cemetery to be found at Cefn Golau, Tredegar.

The plight of the incoming workers did not escape the watchful eye of John Hodder Moggridge, a wealthy Englishman who had settled in Woodfield where he owned a large estate and where he had built a beautiful house. His property included a woodland on the west bank of the river, Y Coed Duon. Around 1820, after discussion with a committee of advisers, he offered grants of land to deserving workers, to build their own homes in an area which he had cleared at his expense. The tenants would be required to pay a regular, reasonable rent, to cover a loan which Moggridge offered to cover the cost of building.

John Moggridge's social experiment was eventually a success after a slow start, initially only three families took up the offer. By 1829, almost three hundred houses had been built and were occupied. A similar plan was carried out at Ynysddu on a smaller scale but with equally encouraging results. Some of the inhabitants of these new communities had the unusual advantage of a reasonably secure and (by the standards of the day) comfortable existence in homes which they had built for themselves. Other houses were built by speculative landlords to be rented out to workers in the various industries that were rapidly creating employment in the area. Many other workers continued to live in primitive huts, in degrading and unsanitary conditions, and utter poverty.

Two of the houses built under John Hodder Moggridge's scheme in Hall Street, Blackwood in the 1830s.

Three quarries in the Blackwood area produced Pennant Sandstone for new buildings. The quarries were at Caerllwyn in the south, Cwm-nant-yr-odyn, southeast of Pontllanfraith and Gelli Quarry at Cwm Gelli, north of Blackwood.

The adjoining areas of the South Wales Coalfield, in the Ebbw Valley, and in the Glamorgan Valleys, were developing at the same time, at an even greater pace in some cases. The importance of the steam coal that was being discovered throughout the coalfield was to bring about an increase in production of 155 - fold between the years 1840 and 1914. It also brought about the development of the railway system throughout the valleys and to the docks at Newport, Cardiff, Barry, Swansea, Llanelli and Port Talbot. The coal of the valleys was found to be ideally suited for use in the ever increasing numbers of steam ships, steam locomotives, and industrial steam engines. It produced maximum steam with comparatively little smoke.

The importance of the quality of the coal that was discovered in the Sirhowy Valley now emerged, the Mynyddislwyn Coal Seam, which was within the Upper Coal Measures that ran throughout the South Wales Coalfield, was extremely valuable and profitable. It was found in the area ranging from Mynyddislwyn Church to Argoed, with a separate patch above Llanhilleth. The coal produced was used mainly for coking, steam coal and housecoal.

Other important coal seams included Big Vein, Elled Vein, Upper and Lower Rhas Las Seams, the Brithdir, and Yard Seams, which were found in different places throughout the area. The coal was accessible at varying depths, throughout the coalfield, ranging from just below the surface of the ground to several hundred feet deep in other areas. The thickness of the seam also varied, from several inches to several feet.

Mining coal was never easy for the colliers of the Sirhowy Valley, who had to contend with difficult geology, and sometimes severe problems of underground flooding, but they persevered not only with great determination, but in desperation. The miners were paid according to the amount of coal they produced, the less they produced the less they could afford to eat. They were not paid for small coal, although inevitably they had to dig out a large quantity of dust and shale to produce the bigger pieces required. They struggled for twelve hours a day in appalling, unsafe and unhealthy conditions to produce as much coal as they could get, to be sure of feeding themselves and their families.

The coal owners were only interested in the end product, coal equalled money. The lives of the workers were in the main, not of any interest. It was cheaper to use people than to use a horse, which had to be purchased. If a man was injured or killed, then another would take his place. The foetid air of the unventilated pits and the regular falls of rock and coal, maimed and killed many. The colliers were treated like slaves, as indeed they were in essence. Slaves were at least housed and fed by their owners, but the miners of the early nineteenth century were not as fortunate. Such small wages as they earned were paid in tokens which had to be spent at the 'Truck Shops', owned by the Coal Owners. The prices were higher than in the markets and once the colliers were in debt, it was impossible to break out of the system. There were several truck shops in the Valley, including those in Argoed, at Blackwood and at the Bryn, in Pontllanfraith.

The coal and iron trades had a series of peaks and depressions during the nineteenth century. In 1830, when trade was at a low ebb, the miners were given reduced wages. They became very agitated, and those in the Crumlin area called a strike. They called for the abolition of the truck system, and a wage in cash of ten shillings (fifty pence) a week. Between two and three thousand workers from the surrounding area attended a meeting at Pentwynmawr, at which Richard Fothergill asked them to put their case. As a result of this meeting, the coal-owners of the district met and decided to agree with the mens' requests and to improve conditions. This example improved conditions slightly in the Valley and in other areas.

CHAPTER THREE

Tredegar continued to develop throughout the first half of the nineteenth century at what must have seemed an amazing pace to both old and new inhabitants. It was a harsh industrial society peopled by men, women and children faced with the bitter realities of the Industrial Revolution that had gripped South Wales.

The average life of a collier was forty years. If he lived long enough, avoiding the terrible accidents that occurred on a daily basis in the mines, he would die of disease due to the conditions in which he lived and worked.

In October 1816 the Tredegar ironworkers went on strike in protest against the reduction in wages; this was the first strike of its kind in South Wales and indicated the pressures that the ironworkers, and also the coal workers, were living under. This was the first of many strikes, although not all were of this scale, and all were against wage reductions, not for increases or improved conditions. Until 1824 trade unions were illegal, and even after 1834 when the Grand Nationalised Consolidated Trades Union set up branches throughout the country, the South Wales ironmasters and coalmasters threatened to sack anyone who joined a Union.

The wild bands of men who called themselves 'Scotch Cattle' operated in the area between 1820 and 1850, gathering in 'Herds' under the leadership of a 'Bull'. Their motive was to fight against wage cuts, and their activities were directed at reducing the output of coal and the number of miners producing it. They did not shrink from the use of intimidation and violence against the workers who did not want to support the Scotch Cattle in the fight against the coalmasters. The workers and the employers all had cause to fear the Cattle.

This turbulent century, marked by poverty, hardship and violence, also created great wealth and prosperity for many people. The conditions were very similar throughout the South Wales coalfield, but still more workers poured in to escape the deprivation they found in rural areas, and the towns of the Valley evolved despite the difficulties of the inhabitants.

The ever increasing demand for coal to feed the expanding ironworks called for a new method of bringing coal to the surface after it had been hewn by the colliers. Known as the whimsey or 'horse gin' this horse-driven machine, which was the forerunner of the winding gear used in modern collieries, was to bring about a massive increase in productivity. This method was used for hauling coal to the surface until 1829 when Evan Davies's Pit in Tredegar, became the first to use water tanks to produce a 'balance pit' in which the surface tank was filled with water to lift a cage at the bottom of the pit. In 1839 No.7, also in Tredegar was the deepest balance pit in Wales, and was some 630 feet (192 metres) in depth. The water balance was only used in South Wales and survived in use for about forty years, until steam engines wound the coal cages up and down the shafts.

In 1841, Upper Ty Trist Colliery was sunk on the site of an old farm in Tredegar. The name of the farm, Ty Trist, means 'House of Sorrow', although the reason for this sad name is unknown.

Several small pits and levels were being worked by this time all along the valley, including Argoed and at Gwrhay, where cottages had been in existence since the 15th century.

The Coach and Horses Inn at Blackwood, historic meeting place of the Chartists.

Pontllanfraith saw the development of shallow coal workings in several places as did the area around Mynyddislwyn. The hamlets which existed in these areas grew into villages as the century progressed.

The area still lacked any form of local government, and the dissatisfaction of the workforce seethed beneath the surface for many years, until in 1839 when the Chartist uprising, in which workers demanded an improved electoral system, brought their feelings into the open. Their Charter was for annual Parliamentary elections, voting rights for men over 21 by secret ballot, 300 constituencies of equal populations, the abolition of the property qualification for Members of Parliament and wages for the MPs.

One of the leaders of the movement, Zephaniah Williams, who was born in Argoed in 1795, worked as a mineral agent at Sirhowy Ironworks. He and his fellow Chartist, John Frost of Newport, held a meeting at the Coach and Horses in Blackwood. A house in the High Street bears a plaque to commemorate the date, 3rd November 1839, when delegates from Fleur-de-Lys, Argoed, and Blackwood and other mining areas met to march on Newport, to meet with further contingents from Tredegar, Rhymney and other mining areas. It is said 'the place was swarming with Chartists'.

In the pouring rain, they marched along the track of the tramway under the command of John Frost, to the Westgate Hotel in Newport, where they were confronted by armed soldiers. Nine of the Chartists were killed by their bullets and forty more, including the leaders John Frost, Zephaniah Williams and William Jones were arrested.

In December 1839 they were tried for high treason at Monmouth, and having been found guilty were sentenced to death, but the sentence was later commuted to transportation to Tasmania. Although the Chartists' march on Newport did not succeed in bringing about immediate improvements in the electoral system, the Chartist movement did have an impact which eventually led to the democratic elections we have today.

Although given their freedom in 1856 after many years in exile, William Jones and Zephaniah Williams preferred to stay in Tasmania, which had become their home, despite the harsh conditions meted out to convicts when they arrived in the colony. John Frost eventually returned, lived into his nineties, and ultimately died in Bristol.

Zephaniah Williams made his fortune in Tasmania as a mine owner and a plaque commemorates his life there as a founder of the Tasmanian Mining Industry, and gives his place of birth as Argoed, South Wales.

In 1840, South Wales coalfields produced two million tons for ironworks, one million for the copper and lime industries and one and a half million tons were exported. Despite all the upheaval of the times, the grinding poverty of the miners, and the difficulties of production, the incessant demand for coal had to be satisfied.

In 1851 the Admiralty issued a report in favour of using South Wales steam coal for the Navy. This increased the value and importance of the coal in the Sirhowy Valley, where coal of excellent quality for engines was to be found in abundance. Various collieries used the term 'ocean', 'naval' or 'navigation' in their names to imply that their coal was the best for ships.

Women were still employed in the mines in the middle of the nineteenth century, for although the Mines Act of 1842 prohibited the employment of women and boys under 10 to work underground, there was little inspection. Women and children were cheap to hire, their families needed the money they earned, so they continued to work pulling skips of coal along the tunnels, and sorting and riddling coal on the surface. Invariably, the women and girls underground worked stripped to the waist and one colliery owner stated that the women worked harder than the slaves in the West Indies.

The small children were employed in the pits to open and close the air doors. They sat at the doors for ten or twelve hours a day, in total darkness, opening them when they could hear the sound of a skip being dragged towards them, and closing the doors when the haulier had passed through. A Royal Commission reported in 1841 that more cases were recorded of the employment of children in pits in South Wales than anywhere else.

Throughout this mid-century period many coal levels were being opened, sometimes being worked on a very small scale by the farmer who owned the land, with the help of a few members of his family. Other workings operated on a bigger scale, with a fairly large workforce.

The need for better transport systems increased with the coal production. John Jones of Llanarth Court owned a large estate of land at Tir-Lewis-David, near Pontllanfraith. He had acquired the estate of Penllwyn Sarph (now known as 'The Penllwyn') through marriage and wanted to exploit the coal he discovered on the 300 acres. The Penllwyn Manor on the estate is now the Hotel.

John Jones and his partner Sir Charles Morgan of the Tredegar Iron Company built the tramroad in 1824. It ran from the Rock Level near Cwm Gelli at Blackwood to Nine Mile Point under the name 'Llanarth Tramroad', the section between Nine Mile Point and Ynysddu was known as the 'Penllwyn Tramroad'.

The Sirhowy Tramroad Company was anxious to protect its business interests and tried to prevent John Jones building his own tramroad. Sir Charles Morgan, although one of the Directors of the Tredegar Iron Company who built the Sirhowy Tramroad, saw the potential of profit from John Jones' tramroad and joined him in a partnership.

The eventual compromise involved the joint ownership of the two tramroad companies in the Penllwyn Tramroad, with the Llanarth Tramroad being owned solely by John Jones and Sir Charles Morgan. Unlike the Sirhowy Tramroad, the trams on the Llanarth and Penllwyn Tramroads were always pulled by horses, no steam locomotives were used.

The route from Cwm Gelli, Blackwood ran past the 'Rock and Fountain Inn' which is reputed to be the original counting house and weighing office for the Llanarth and Penllwyn tramroads, and other notable surviving features are the river bridge at Nine Mile Point and the Crooked Bridge at Gelligroes (Pont Gam).

William Lewis Meredith's book, 'The Tramroads of the Sirhowy Valley', written in 1907, lists the tramroads:
1. The Monmouthshire Canal Company Tramroad from Newport.
2. The Sirhowy Main Tramroad from Nine Mile Point to the Sorrwy Furnaces and the Cwm Gelli branches near Blackwood.
3. The Penllwyn Branch from Nine Mile Point to Ynysddu.
4. The Bryn Tramroad from the Sirhowy Tramroad to a junction about four and a half miles from Nine Mile Point to the village of Bryn, and thence to Gelli-haf Coal Level.
5. The Llanarth Tramway from the junction with the Sirhowy Tramroad at Ynysddu to the Rock Coal Level at Charles-town, Blackwood.

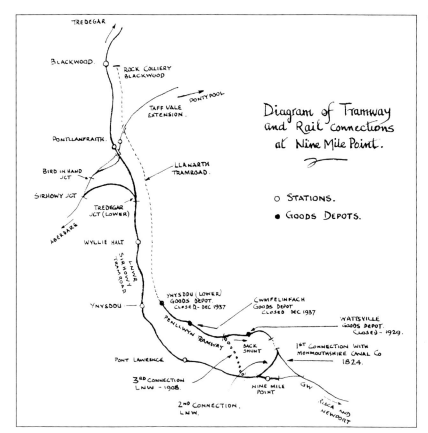

The Llanarth and Penllwyn Tramroads ran from The Rock Level at Blackwood to Nine Mile Point.

A photograph taken in 1995 of the Rock and Fountain Inn, Blackwood which was reputed to be the weighing and counting house for the Llanarth & Penllwyn tramroad.

The river bridge at Gelligroes with the Mill in the background.

The Mill at Gelligroes, a favourite place of Islwyn the poet.

The Babell Chapel where 'Islwyn' is buried.

John Jones employed a mineral agent, Morgan Thomas, who lived in Ty'r Agent (The Agent's House) built alongside the tramroad at Ynysddu. It was there that his ninth child was born, William Thomas, on 3rd April 1832. William Thomas grew up to to be the poet 'Islwyn' who took his bardic name from the Mynydd Islwyn, to demonstrate his love for his homeland and all things Welsh. The family moved to a larger house at Cwmfelinfach in 1854, and in 1859 'Islwyn' was ordained. Although never given a church, he was a popular preacher in several churches in the Valley, including the Babell Chapel.

Although his family were English-speaking, he studied Welsh with the help of his brother-in-law and his friend Aneurin Ffard, the miller at Gelligroes, who helped him to understand and appreciate Welsh poetry. Several of his later poems were written at the Mill, and having won four Bardic Chairs at Eisteddfodau between 1870 and 1877, he has since been renowned as a Welsh language poet. Islwyn died on 20 November 1878 at the age of 46, leaving a widow, Martha. He is buried at the Babell Chapel in Cwmfelinfach, where he loved to live and preach. During his short life, Islwyn had seen his beloved Valley change almost beyond his belief. The once peaceful woodlands had been diminished, and all around were coalworkings in varying stages of development and production.

The Sirhowy Tramroad was in regular use by two more steam locomotives in addition to Britannia. Trams became derailed or the track broke down, these were regular occurrences throughout the length of the line. In 1860 the tramway had been converted to a standard gauge single line railway and an Act of 1860 changed the name of the owning Company to the Sirhowy Railway Company.

The new railway was re-routed from Sirhowy to Blackwood by going behind the line of the houses, so avoiding the High Streets of Blackwood and Argoed. The Monmouthshire line from Nine Mile Point to Newport was completed as a Railway in 1855 and the Sirhowy Railway was granted running powers when the Monmouthshire Railway and Canal Co. started its passenger service in June 1865 to Newport (Dock Street).

The trains consisted of 3 four-wheel coaches, with 2-4-0 tank engines and offered first, second and third class fares. The journey from Sirhowy to Newport took 1 hour and 20 minutes on average, and called en-route at Tredegar, Blackwood, Tredegar Junction and Risca.

Argoed Station was opened in 1866, followed by Nine Mile Point Station in 1867. By 1870 three passenger trains from the Sirhowy Valley were terminating at Newport High Street, the freight trains continuing to bring increasing tonnage to the docks.

The other railway into the Sirhowy Valley was adapted from the Hall's Road Tramroad, which had been built between 1805 and 1814 by Benjamin Hall, the son-in-law of Richard Crawshay the Cyfartha Ironmaster. Benjamin Hall was the father of Sir Benjamin Hall, who later became Lord Llanover, the Chief Commissioner of Works for the Houses of Parliament. Sir Benjamin Hall commissioned the clock on the Tower, which was named 'Big Ben' after him.

The Hall's Road Tramroad ran through the Western Valley from Cross Keys, and turning sharply west at Pentwynmawr, continued to Waterloo Colliery in Gwrhay in 1811 and to Manmoel Level in 1814, where it served the collieries in the area. Halls Road was eventually taken over and became part of the Great Western Railway.

Another important feature of the railway system in the Valley was the Taff Vale extension, which in the 1860s formed a junction at two points with the Sirhowy Railway at Pontllanfraith. From 1865 the Great Western Railway coal traffic from the Taff Valley used this extension from Pontllanfraith and along the Sirhowy Railway to Newport.

The coming of the railways opened up the steamcoal coalfield, enabling freight and passengers to enter and leave the Valley by linked railway networks which were being built all over the country.

In 1873 the newly created Tredegar Iron and Coal Company took over the Tredegar Iron Company which had made such an impact in the iron producing area at the northern end of the Valley. Familiarly known as 'The T.I.C.' it was instrumental in making Tredegar an 'Iron Town', the Town Clock which still stands in the centre of the town commemorates the importance of the iron works. The Company, which was always progressive, realised that its success was now centred on its valuable coal property and changed its focus of activities.

The Sirhowy Ironworks at Tredegar in the late 19th century.

The Tredegar Iron and Coal Company offices in Tredegar, still in use in 1996 as the premises of a local manufacturing company.

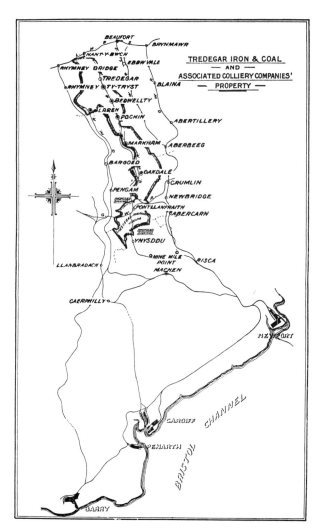

A 1920s map of the Tredegar Iron and Coal Company's property in the Sirhowy and Rhymney Valleys.

The names of some of the important collieries which the Company eventually owned is reflected in this list of Directors, names which became famous in the industrial life of the country:

Isaac Lowthian Bell	William Newmarch	Edward Williams
William Menelaus	Sidney Carr Glyn	James Wyllie
Henry Davis Pochin	Benjamin Whitworth	Charles Markham

An artist's impression of Tredegar town clock shortly after its completion in 1859. The clock tower which is 72 feet (22 metres) high and made of cast iron was originally manufactured at the Charles Jordan Iron Foundry at Newport. It was provided for the convenience of the workers in the nearby Sirhowy and Tredegar Ironworks and the collieries at Ty Trist and Bedwellty. This local landmark is a symbolic reminder of Tredegar's historic past as a major iron manufacturing town.

Probably photographed in the 1920s is the 19th century Engine Pit at Sirhowy, Tredegar. Some 80 coal workings are known to have been operating in Tredegar during the halcyon days of the last century.

Bedwellty House, situated in Bedwellty Park, Tredegar. This was built in 1818 by Samuel Homfray, ironmaster, on the site of a former farmhouse Ty Lodwig Rees. The house and park were presented to the people of Tredegar in 1901.

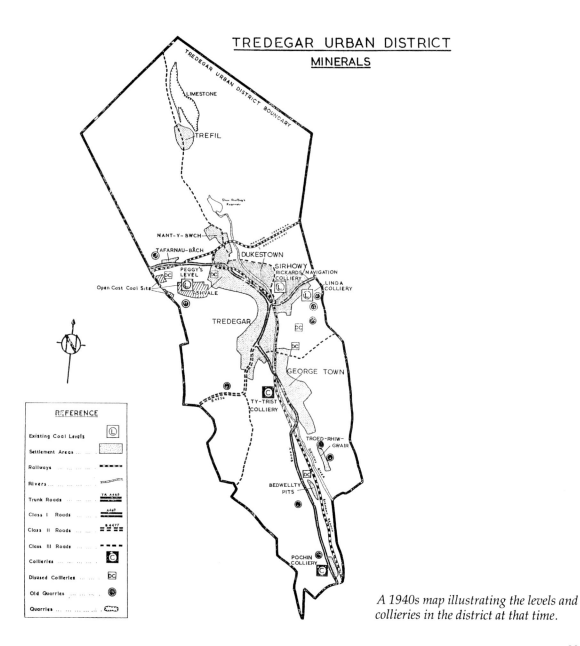

TREDEGAR URBAN DISTRICT
MINERALS

LIMESTONE

TREFIL

Shon Sheffrey's Reservoir

NANT-Y-BWCH

TAFARNAU-BACH

DUKESTOWN

SIRHOWY

PEGGY'S LEVEL

RICKARDS NAVIGATION COLLIERY

Open Cast Coal Site

ASHVALE

LINDA COLLIERY

TREDEGAR

GEORGE TOWN

TY-TRIST COLLIERY

TROED-RHIW-GWAIR

BEDWELLTY PITS

POCHIN COLLIERY

REFERENCE

Existing Coal Levels	ⓛ
Settlement Areas	
Railways	
Rivers	
Trunk Roads	TR A465
Class I Roads	A469
Class II Roads	B 4477
Class III Roads	
Collieries	ⓒ
Disused Collieries	ⅅⅭ
Old Quarries	⊙
Quarries	

A 1940s map illustrating the levels and collieries in the district at that time.

BLACKWOOD & PONTLLANFRAITH AREA
MINERALS

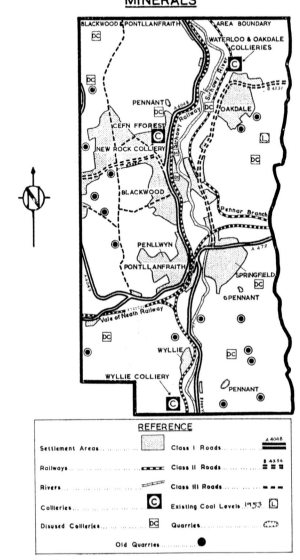

A 1940s map showing quarries and collieries.

CHAPTER FOUR

Travelling from the northern end of the Valley to the south, several major collieries which were sunk in the nineteenth century, were still operational in the twentieth century.

Ty Trist at the southern end of Tredegar dated from 1834, when its two pits were sunk to serve the Tredegar Iron Works, was to remain in production for a total of 125 years until 1959. The colliery was a group of pits which also included Upper Ty Trist, sunk in 1841 and Number 3 Ty-Trist which was sunk in 1868.

The Ty-Trist and the adjacent Whitworth Collieries were linked to form one extensive coal mine, which worked the Elled Seam and the Old Coal Seam. In 1873, when the Tredegar Iron Company became the Tredegar Iron and Coal Company, in recognition of its greater interest in coal production, Ty-Trist was one of the company's twenty collieries in the Tredegar area that underwent a modernisation scheme. Throughout its long life the colliery was used to test many new innovations in coal mining, including one of the finest washeries in South Wales, which was installed in 1892. In 1910 the workforce totalled 1220, and by the time the National Coal Board had taken over in 1947, it was the only remaining Tredegar Iron Company pit still in existence and probably the oldest pit in South Wales to be incorporated by nationalisation.

A few miles south of Ty-Trist, Pochin Colliery was also still working until closure in 1964, having been sunk in 1876. Pochin was named after Miss Laura Pochin, daughter of Henry Pochin, one of the directors of the Tredegar Iron and Coal Company, she later married Lord Aberconwy, who was the Company Chairman.

Pochin was an extensive 340 yard (311 metres) deep pit, which employed 1696 men in 1910. Built to the most modern standards of the time, the facilities included the first air compressor, which was installed in 1893 and a washery in 1897.

Both Ty-Trist and Pochin benefited by the introduction of endless rope haulage, and were lit by electricity by the end of the nineteenth century. Despite these innovations, the Tredegar Iron and Coal Company reported the number of horses still in use was 626 in 1923 compared with 287 in the first year of the Company's existence.

Pochin Village, which consisted of one short row of houses, was built for some of its workers, but others travelled from Tredegar and other places on the Pochin colliers' train. After the First World War in 1918, more than 13,000 men were employed in the Tredegar Pits.

Bedwellty Pits came into existence in 1850. Houses were built in the village for the colliers who worked there. About the same time, the village of Troedrhiwgwair was built, high on the mountain slopes above the river, to house the people who worked in the nearby coal workings. The Elled, Big Vein and Yard Seams were worked in this area.

Hollybush was named after a local wood, the colliery was sunk near to the site of Pantymila Farm, where there had been an old coal level. The Old and New Hollybush Levels were served by the colliery shaft, working the Pontygwaith Seam, also known as the Brithdir Seam, which was house coal. The owner, E.D.Williams, was High Sheriff of Monmouthshire, he owned other

A view of Tredegar Station with its locomotive shed during the 1920s. On the right is Whitworth Colliery and Ty-Trist is to the left.

collieries including one at Argoed. In 1890 he built his beautiful house, 'Maesrudded', which is now the Maes Manor Hotel. The village of Hollybush grew around the colliery at the same time, the colliery being operational from about 1880 to the 1920s.

Abernant Colliery, sunk in 1880 had two shafts, West and East. It was owned by the Bargoed Coal Company and was built near the bridge in the Argoed area, called Pont-Abernant-y-felin, and named in full after the bridge. One of the best smith's coal was produced in this mine, and in 1890 one thousand bags were sent to different consignees all over the country to advertise the fact. The colliery was worked for over fifty years and was linked underground to Llanover Colliery.

In 1929, Llanover Colliery, one mile south of Markham, originally owned by Bargoed Coal Company, was taken over by the Tredegar Iron and Coal Company and production of coal having ceased, it was put into service as a pumping station to reduce the water pressure on the coal barrier between Llanover Colliery and the Oakdale pits. Llanover which was named after the Llanover Estate, was sunk in 1909 and coal from the pit, when it was producing, was carried over Hall's Road into the Western Valley.

Number Nine colliery, later Graham's Navigation Colliery, was originally an Ebbw Vale Company pit.

Ty-Trist before the screens were built in 1925. This colliery was the oldest to be nationalised in 1947.

Ty Trist office staff and others firing the boilers at Ty Trist Colliery during the strike in 1921.
From left to right: Harold Selby, Boss of outside labourers. Harry Andrews, Surveyors' Department, General Offices. Fred Thomas, Mechanic, Ty Trist. Man in cap - unknown. Walter Jones, Drawing Office, General Offices.

An early photograph of miners before the days of helmets.

Alice James, B.E.M. who worked at Ty Trist hauling trams as a young girl, and then as a cleaner/general worker. Photographed in 1949 by Mr Derek L. Harding.

The one-time industrious scene at Tredegar Station which opened for business in the year 1865. The last passenger train was to leave the town in June 1960.

Another once familiar spectacle was the colliery steam engine. This locomotive, named 'Sir Charles Allen' is seen performing some shunting work at Whitworth Colliery, probably during the 1950s.

A passenger train at Tredegar awaits commencement of its journey down the Sirhowy Valley to Newport. No. 6426 was a former Great Western Railway steam locomotive and this picture dates from the late 1950s.

The camerman has well captured this wintry scene with the men trudging alongside the trams during a chilly shift at Ty Trist in 1954.

The men make their way home after a hard day's work at Ty Trist on June 6th 1956.

These surface photographs at Ty Trist illustrate the tumbler flow. The trams would convey the coal to the tumblers and to the awaiting screens as seen in the lower picture.

A fine view overlooking Ty Trist Colliery and the neighbouring rows of houses as they all appeared more than 70 years ago in 1921.

To be compared with the photograph on the previous page is the same scene as pictured in 1995. Completely vanished, is all evidence of the colliery that once flourished here until 1959 and the site has now been transformed to one of leisure and sport.

Ty Trist as photographed in 1954 shows it to be a typical mid 19th century colliery layout.

Little did they realise at the time but these pit ponies were photographed during their very last day toiling at Ty Trist Colliery. The surface buildings in the background which may be remembered by former workers are the offices, No.1 winder, fire room, together with the carpenters, blacksmiths and fitting shops.

A typical day inside the fitting shop in 1953 when part of the 'Slusher', underground machinery is under repair.

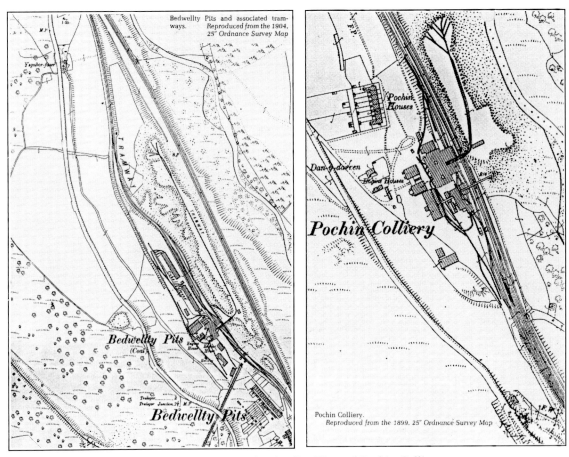

Some early Ordnance Maps showing the sites of Bedwellty Pits and Pochin Colliery.

THE LATE EXPLOSION AT THE TREDEGAR COLLIERY : SCENE AT THE PIT-HEAD AFTER THE ACCIDENT.

Taken from the Illustrated London News is this tragic scene witnessed at Bedwellty Pits in June 1865 following the explosion which claimed the lives of 26 men.

Two photographs of the Bedwellty Collieries taken during the early 1900s. The pits first commenced production in the year 1857 and the village of Bedwellty Pits grew around these once prosperous colliery workings.

A nostalgic scene at Bedwellty Pits Halt in August 1950 as the 1.10pm from Newport is hauled by an ex LNWR 0-6-2T locomotive No. 58933.

The spartan coaches of the colliers train seen at Bedwellty.

This is a fine example of a 19th century haulage drum which had survived on the mountainside above the site of the former Bedwellty Pits and photographed during the 1990s.

(Ready for Work)
.Pochin Colliers, Having a Woodbine, Before Descending Pit, .98.

Pochin colliers ready for work at the turn of this century with a very apt inscription on the original photograph.

Colliers entering Bond at Pochin Pit, Nr. Tredegar

Pochin colliers entering pit cage (bond).

Both of these photographs of Pochin Colliery were taken from almost the same location. On the left is a perspective from the 1950s, displaying a hive of activity and industrialisation. Below, and some forty years later, in 1995, the reclaimers and landscapers have done their work and green fields and trees have returned to this part of the valley.

Pochin Colliery, Near Tredegar, Mon.

Pochin Colliery near Tredegar during the early 1920s. The photograph above reveals that the downcast shaft has a then new 'lattice' type of headframe whilst the upcast is of a much earlier timber construction.

Pochin Colliery as viewed from the south. Pochin worked from the 1880s until final closure in 1965.

The end of a day shift at Pochin and the workers are photographed whilst waiting for the 3.50 pm train to take them home to Tredegar.

Another select view of Pochin Colliery, this time looking east and dating from the 1950s.

Hollybush Colliery. The Hollybush Colliery encompassed both old and new levels and worked from 1888 to 1921.

Hollybush Station during L.N.W.R. days.

IN CHANCERY.
MONMOUTHSHIRE.

HOLLYBUSH COLLIERY AND COKE WORKS.

MESSRS. FULLER, HORSEY, SON, and CO. are instructed by the Official Liquidator, with the approbation of the Master of the Rolls, to SELL BY AUCTION, on FRIDAY, October 9, at Two o'clock precisely, at the WESTGATE HOTEL, NEWPORT. Monmouthshire, in One Lot, the Valuable LEASEHOLD MINERAL PROPERTY, known as the "HOLLY BUSH COLLIERY and COKE WORKS," with the Fixed and Loose Plant, Machinery, Rolling Stock, Loose Tools, and Stores, situate in the Parish of Bedwelty, in the County of Monmouth, about 17 miles from the shipping port of Newport, and in direct communication therewith by the Sirhowy Railway, which has a siding to the pit's mouth and coke ovens.

The total area of the Mineral Property is about 79 Acres, containing a Seam of Coal called the Pontygwaith and Marshall's Vein, about 2ft 8in. in thickness, well adapted for household and coking purposes. The colliery is held at rents and royalties. There are 55 Large Coking Ovens, a Ten-horse-Power Steam Engine, with Winding Gear and Headstocks, Cast and Wrought Iron Tramways, 33 Iron and Wood Tram Waggons, Coke Barrows, Miners' and Smiths' Tools, Three Double purchase Crabs, &c.

May be viewed previous to the Sale, and full particulars obtained from F. WHINNEY, Esq., Official Liquidator, No. 8, Old Jewry, E.C ; TUFNELL SOUTHGATE, Esq., Solicitor, 7, King's-bench-Walk, Temple, E.C. ; at the WESTGATE and KING'S HEAD HOTELS, Newport ; and of Messrs. FULLER, HORSEY, SON, and CO., 11, Billiter Square, London, E.C. [12,808

Hollybush Colliery Notice of Sale which appeared in the Monmouthshire Merlin.

A miner's payslip dated 15 May 1915. Note the total gross pay of £7.14.5 (£7.72). Including a special 'War Bonus' of £1.34).

60

Pictured at Hollybush in August 1959, a former Great Western Railway 0-6-0 PT locomotive No. 6426 coupled to a single carriage is about to depart for Tredegar.

Miners and officials pictured at Hollybush Colliery with their safety lamps but with a distinct lack of safety headgear. This being an extremely early photograph, probably dates from the 1880s.

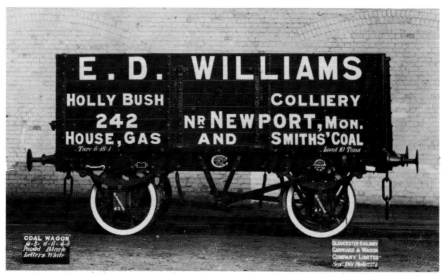

One of the many privately owned wagons used in the Sirhowy Valley.

Markham Colliery was sunk between the years 1910 and 1913, about four miles south of Tredegar, with two shafts North and South, sunk to 600 yards (549 metres), to work the Big Vein Seam. Again it was owned by a subsidiary of the TIC, the Markham Steam Coal Company, named after Sir Arthur Basil Markham, son of Charles Markham, a director of TIC. Sir Arthur's grandfather was Sir Joseph Paxton, designer of the great Industrial Exhibition of 1851 and the Crystal Palace, built in London in 1853.

Sir Arthur Markham was a greatly respected figure in the mining circles in which he worked, in the Midlands as well as in South Wales. He became a director of the Tredegar Iron and Coal Company, the Oakdale Colliery Company, as well as chairman of the Markham Steam Coal Company. He was considered to be innovative, almost ahead of his time in his quest for the most up to date plant and machinery, and it was he who initiated the use of electricty in the mines, which made the Tredegar Iron and Coal Company pioneers among the South Wales Coal owners. Sir Arthur was also interested in providing better living conditions for coal workers, and he was instrumental in ensuring that the villages of both Oakdale and Markham were well designed.

Markham Colliery 1976.

In 1900 Sir Arthur Markham was elected to Parliament as the Liberal Member for Mansfield, in Nottingham. In one of his speeches in the House of Commons, he said that never a week passed in which he did not go down a pit. He said *'I have worked with miners, played with them, fought with them, aye, and carried out their dead bodies with my own hands.'*

Markham Colliery remained operational for many years, providing work for many generations of men, but the coal reserves were eventually worked out and the pit closed in 1985.

Markham Colliery in about 1958, a pit which saw production last for more than 70 years until closure in 1985.

Seen at Markham in 1956 is this railway crew comprising of Mr Lyn Williams (Guard), Mr Geoff Rowlands (Driver) and Mr John Taylor (Fireman). The locomotive, No. 49409 was the last London and North Western Railway Company's engine to work in the Sirhowy Valley.

Markham Colliery was linked to Oakdale Colliery in World War 2 to provide a way out in case of bombing and also in 1979 when output was diverted to Oakdale.

Abernant Colliery 1880-1932 was linked underground to Llanover Colliery. Abernant produced fine smith's coal.

The site of the former Abernant Colliery as it appeared in a photograph taken in 1990.

Llanover Colliery, Argoed. Nr Blackwood. 409

Llanover Colliery,
originally owned by the
Bargoed Coal Co. This was
taken over by the Tredegar
Iron and Coal Co. Ltd in
1929/30 for use as a
pumping station to relieve
pressure on the coal barrier
between Llanover and
Oakdale. The original
steam pumps were replaced
in 1932 by electrically
driven Sulzer Deepwell
Pumps each with a capacity
of 150,000 gallons per hour.

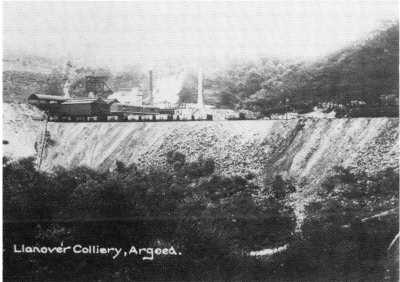

Llanover Colliery, Argoed.

A coal company
delivery note for customer
Mr. A.T. Tasker,
stationmaster at
Markham 1920-1933.

69

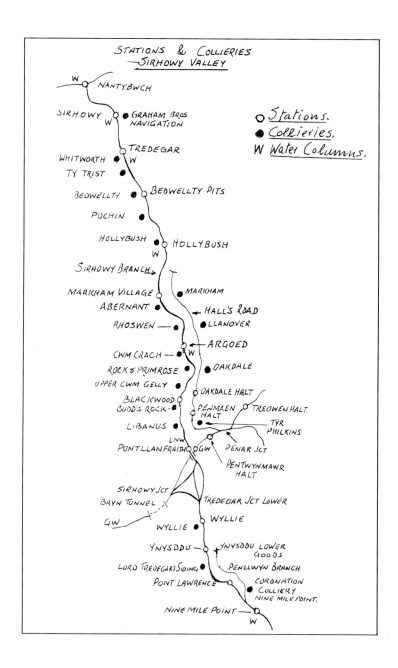

This interesting map was marked out by Mr. W.W. Tasker and is reproduced with his kind permission.

A Newport to Tredegar train passing Rhoswen sidings Argoed. The locomotive is a L.N.W.R. coal tank and the photograph was taken in L.M.S. days circa 1935.

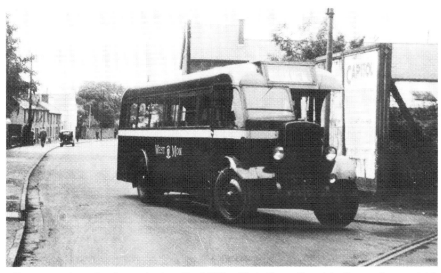

A West Mon Bus turns into the depot during the 1950s. Note the rails set in the roadway which marked the crossing from Blackwood Station into Budds Colliery sidings.

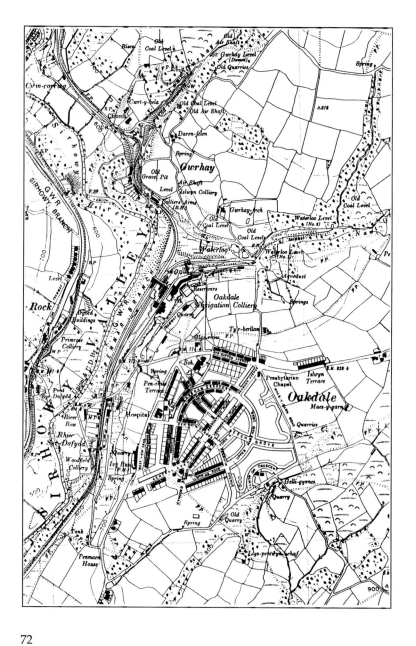

Oakdale village was developed by the Tredegar Iron and Coal Co. for workers at Oakdale and Waterloo Collieries.

In 1907 the Tredegar Iron and Coal Company, through its subsidiary, Oakdale Navigation Collieries Ltd. began the sinking of Oakdale Navigation, on land which was originally owned by the Tredegar and Llanover estates, on the eastern bank of the Sirhowy River. It was near the site of Woodfield House, which had been built for John Hodder Moggeridge, one of the founders of Blackwood. The acquisition of this land gave the Company a continuous mineral area in the Sirhowy Valley which extended for ten miles from its first coal workings. Oakdale was the name of a local wood.

Oakdale was to be the first of three modern collieries to be built by the Tredegar Iron and Coal Company. It had three shafts, North Pit, South Pit, and Waterloo Pit. It provided electric power for its own workings, plus those of Markham and Wyllie Collieries which were sunk later.

The adjacent Waterloo Colliery, sunk in 1908, produced House Coal, and was assimilated into the Oakdale Colliery site, where it became a Mines Training Centre. This colliery was on the site of the old Waterloo Level, first exploited by the Tredegar Iron Company in 1815, and named after the battle. It was connected to Islwyn Colliery, which worked the Brithdir Seam.

Waterloo Pit. Waterloo Colliery 1908-1970 was a House Coal Pit it later became a Mines Training Centre.

December 16th 1931 saw a Royal visitor to Oakdale, that of HRH Prince George.

Oakdale Colliery, Blackwood.

By 1930, Oakdale was producing one million tons of coal, with a manpower of 2,000. It was linked to Markham in 1979, and Celynon North in 1981. It thus became the largest and last deep colliery in Gwent when it closed in 1989.

Oakdale Colliery also had a totally new concept for housing the workers of the modern colliery, with well-designed housing built away from the works amid green fields, for its workers and their families.

Ralph Thomas, in his book 'Oakdale, a Model Village' writes:

'It was not to be the usual collection of houses surrounding the pit, with all the disadvantages of similar schemes in the coal mining areas of South Wales. No terraces of houses climbing the side of the valley in which the colliery was to be built. Unlike the terraced houses of the Rhondda and Merthyr, thrown up to meet the demand, the theme for Oakdale was completely original in both design and amenities.

The idea for the modern colliery with its attendant village, was the brainchild of the then managing director of the Tredegar Iron and Coal Co., Mr A.S. Tallis. Of the three collieries planned in the area, Oakdale was the first to be developed. Each was to have its Model Village and it is strange that Markham Colliery and Village, just a few years behind Oakdale in development, did not receive the same attention.'

The roof supports in this underground photograph of Oakdale in the 1920s were made of iron rings manufactured by the Tredegar Iron and Coal Company.

Pit bottom at Oakdale 1920s. Note how high the coal is raised above the top of the tram.

Oakdale Colliery M20 Face circa 1981-82. Front Row: Elwyn Thomas (Team Captain), Brian Coyle (Chocker), Graham Williams (Overman). Back row: Trainee, name unknown, Jack Williams (Cutterman).

Waterloo Colliery showing the lift that was installed to carry the men between the pithead and the baths.

On the left is an unusual photograph taken at Oakdale sometime in 1957 when a tram fell down the shaft and wrecked the cage.

This photograph and that on the following page were taken during an Oakdale Colliery trip to the Wye Valley and Tintern in about 1958. A few familiar faces to be recognised by fellow miners are: J. Cordell, Sonny Morris, B. Daniels, D. Williams, Bill Williams, G. Windsor, J. Badham, Les Williams, Ron Radford, J. Urin, G. Jones, G. Oliver, J. Bloxham, Doc Rees, J. Smallcombe and Ray Hoskins.

Again, the daytrippers from Oakdale take a break during their outing to the Wye Valley. The conductress is Connie, surrounded amongst others by J. Cordell, Sonny Morris, B. Daniels, D. Williams, Ray Hoskins, Bill Williams, G. Windsor, J. Badham, Les Williams and Ron Radford.

The North Shaft of Oakdale pictured shortly after the pit's closure in 1989 with Rock Villas in the background.

Oakdale Colliery circa 1970 showing Waterloo Colliery shaft on the left and the two Oakdale shafts.

A view across the Oakdale site in 1995 and readers will need to compare this with the photograph on page 82 to witness the transformation. Rock Villas are still to be seen in the background.

BLACKWOOD & PONTLLANFRAITH AREA
HISTORIC DEVELOPMENT

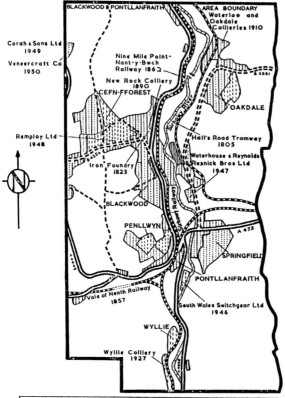

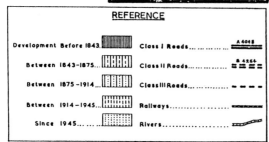

This 1940s map shows Nine Mile Point to Nant-y-Bwch Railway, the Sirhowy Railway, the Vale of Neath Railway and Hall's Road Tramway plus several other major employers of the time.

Budd's Rock Colliery.

Several smaller pits also came into existence in the valley, including Budd's Rock Colliery, sunk about 1880 in the Blackwood area, which was actually a group of collieries, including Rock Pit, New Rock and Rock Levels. The colliery closed in 1957.

BUDD and Co.

Proprietors of the ABERBEEG COLLIERY

(Late Henry Powell),

First-Class Large, Thro' and Thro', and Small Bunker Coal (clean-burning durable and of high calorific power). Worked Thro' and Thro' a Speciality.

Also Proprietors of ROCK, PLAS, ARGOED & CWM-GELLI COLLIERIES
Celebrated Mynyddislwyn House, Gas, Smithy, and
Coking Coals.   ::   ::   Bunker Coal.

Exporters of all descriptions of Cardiff and Newport Steam, House,
Smithy and Anthracite Coals.   ::   :.   Coke and Patent Fuel.
Importers of Pitwood.

Dowlais Chambers, CARDIFF ; and NEWPORT, Mon.

Although the photograph shows Budd's Aberbeeg Colliery in the Western Valley, it is included here to illustrate the company's other activities at The Rock, Plas, Argoed and Cwm-Gelli Collieries in the Sirhowy Valley.

86

A train loaded with coal is seen reversing into the sidings at Pontllanfraith in September 1954.

The site of the level crossing at Pontllanfraith High Level Station. The signal box was on the right and this is the scene as we know it today. (Photograph 1996)

Pontllanfraith Low Level Station which was situated on the Pontypool Road to Aberdare and Swansea Line. The bridge in the background carried the main Newport to Tredegar Road. The picture is from the 1950s, as evidenced by a fashionable Ford car of the day, seen parked near the station buildings.

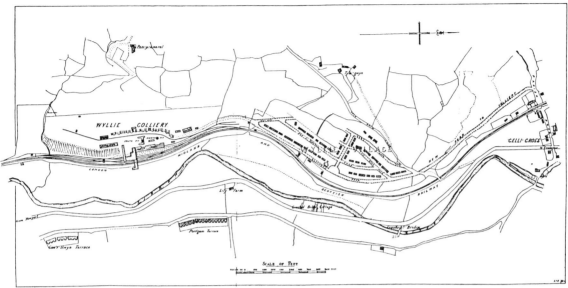

FIG. 1.—GENERAL ARRANGEMENT OF COLLIERY AND VILLAGE.

An informative map showing the layout of Wyllie Colliery and surrounding village during the 1920s.

The third Tredegar Iron and Coal Company colliery in the valley, (whose proprietors Tredegar (Southern) Collieries Ltd, a subsidiary of TIC) was that of Wyllie. North Pit and South Pit, were sunk between 1924 and 1926 and worked until 1968. Wyllie Village was also constructed at this time to house the workers.

The colliery and the village were named after Lt. Colonel Alexander Keith Wyllie, who was born in Liverpool in 1853. He was a barrister by profession and became a director of both the Tredegar Companies and the Oakdale Colliery. He was a gallant soldier in the South African War 1900-1902 and was awarded medals for his actions.

Some fellow workmates pictured at Wyllie Colliery.
Back Row (left to right): Graham Rogers, Ron Jones (Blacksmith), David Lewis (Electrician). Front Row: Eddie Cousens (Banksman), Wyndham Williams (Fitter), Bill Price (Welder), Dennis Jones (Ropeway) and Bob Price (Security).

Wyllie Colliery 1926-1968.

Wyllie Colliery was a highly mechanised operation from the earliest years of production during the 1920s. Whilst there was still much man-handling of the coal output at most of the other local pits, Wyllie was provided with modern machine cutters and conveyor systems. Both of the pictures on this page were taken shortly after the closure of 1968. The photograph on the left has an added interest in that amongst the colliery workings, the photographer has managed to capture a 'Hawk' in his lens! By careful study, can the reader locate this bird of prey?

Wyllie Colliery 1968. The colliery had North and South Shafts and was electrically supplied mainly from Oakdale Colliery.

Nine Mile Point Colliery probably mid 1950s.

Nine Mile Point Colliery with some miners' family members in the foreground.

Nine Mile Point Colliery 1902-1964 was originally owned by Burnyeat and Brown.

In July 1902, alongside the Penllwyn Tramroad, between Cwmfelinfach and Wattsville, the sinking began of Nine Mile Point Colliery, originally called Coronation Colliery and owned by Burnyeat and Brown at that time. A survey had revealed that 225 million tons of coal existed in the area between Cross Keys and Pontllanfraith, and an article in the Western Mail suggested that the Sirhowy Valley might be developed into a second Rhondda. The colliery was sunk with two shafts, West Pit, 392 yards (358 metres) deep, and East Pit 383 (350 metres) yards deep but during the sinking in August 1904, almost at the end of the shift, a fall of rock buried 26 men, killing seven of them. In 1908, a third shaft, Rock Vein Pit was sunk, to a depth of 203 (186 metres) yards.

South Wales Echo

& Evening Express

SIXTH
EDITION

No. 16,175   Estab. 50 Years.   ONE PENNY.

THURSDAY, OCTOBER 17, 1935.

STAY-IN STRIKERS DEFY FED

NINE MILE POINT,
CWMPARC & GARW
MEN STILL IN PITS

*"Will Not Leave Until Rival
Union Workers Clear Out"*

OFFICIALS' VAIN PLEA

*Risca and Rhondda Miners
Up: Some Resume
Work To-day*

" Stay-in " miners at the Nine Mile Point,
Dare, Cwmparc, Parc No. 2 and the Ocean
Garw Valley collieries have refused to leave the
pits, despite the advice of the Federation Executive
Committee to do so.

Federation officials spent an hour in the three pits comprising the Nine Mile Point Colliery, but the men remained adamant.

It is stated that they are determined to remain below
until the owners' verbal agreement to employ only Federation men is translated to black and white, while the men in
the Cwmparc and Garw pits declare their determination to

A South Wales Echo article of October 17 1935.

Nine Mile Point Colliery, Newport with relatives and friends waiting at the pit-head for news of the miners who are conducting a stay-in strike below. The 1935 stay down strike was supported by miners at Risca Pit and other collieries.

The famous 'stay down strike' was in 1935, when about 190 of the colliers refused to leave the three pits in a protest against the use of miners who were not members of the South Wales Miners Federation, to which the miners of the Nine Mile Point Colliery belonged. Further down the valley, 200 men at Risca Pit stayed down in sympathy, as did others in the valley and other areas. Feelings ran high, and in all about 2,000 miners were supporting the 'stay-down', whilst on the surface, a train carrying 70 non-Federation miners back to Merthyr was stoned near Wyllie. The men spent 177 hours underground, returning to the surface only after they had been promised that no non-Federation men would be employed.

When Nine Mile Point closed in 1964, all that remained was a huge waste tip that rose 140 feet (43 metres) high from the valley floor and seemed likely to engulf the Babell Chapel. The tip was removed in the 1970s and the site is now the Nine Mile Point Industrial Estate.

Pit bottom at Nine Mile Point showing rows of trams and the overhead haulage cables.

Conveyor transfer point underground at Nine Mile Point. Note timber props supporting the roof in this old photograph.

The village of Wattsville came into existence late in the nineteenth century, to provide housing for the workers in several collieries in the area, including Nine Mile Point and Risca. The village was named after Edmund Hannay Watts who formed the London and South Wales Coal Company in 1873. This company had sunk the North Risca Pits in 1875 and, as the Abercarn Coal Company Ltd, reopened the Abercarn Colliery in 1885. The two groups amalgamated with other groups in 1895 to form the United National Collieries Ltd. of which Edmund Watts was Chairman.

Edmund Watts was also much involved in the collieries of the Rhondda and the town of Wattstown is named after him. He was born in Northumberland in 1830, of Scottish descent. He became involved in cargo shipping and with his partner became leading merchant ship owners of the nineteenth century, being the first to use steam ships on the London - Australia trade route. This interest, clearly linked to an appreciation of the steam coal produced in the South Wales Valleys, led Edmund Watts to the Sirhowy and Rhondda and into coal ownership.

Eventually, his company owned thirty steamships and the entire output of the United Collieries at Risca and Wattstown went to them. Although Edmund Watts never lived in Wales, some of his eight children did, his daughter Emily married the Revd. W.M. Munro of Newport, and her father built and endowed All Saints Church in Brynglas Road in celebration of their marriage.

Blackvein Colliery, also known as the Old Blackvein Colliery, was owned by John Russell and Co. in 1836, when the coal was discovered to be ideal steam coal, giving little smoke and waste. The coal produced was used by the steamships of the P & O Line, the East Indies Co. and the Royal West Indian Steam Packet. The site covered over 1,000 acres and in addition to working the old Blackvein, worked the Rock Vein which was also steam coal, the Sun Vein, which was house coal and the Big Vein which was industrial coal.

Risca Colliery, near Crosskeys, originally owned by the London and South Wales Colliery Company, had two shafts sunk to the Black Vein Seam in 1878. The old Black Vein Colliery which it replaced had a tragic record of disaster, which seemed to continue when on the 15th July 1880, an explosion killed 120 men. Another accident almost two years later killed four more colliers. The United National Coal Co. and later the Ocean Coal Co. continued in production until the National Coal Board took over in 1947. The colliery closed in 1967.

These two important collieries were for many years major employers in the area, which also had many other thriving industries including several limestone quarries, iron and copper works and other metal trades.

Illustration from 'London Illustrated News' of relatives at the Pit Head of the Old Blackvein Colliery in 1880 when 120 men were killed in the mine.

100

Risca North Colliery, which had an exceptionally long life span of 89 years, had two shafts which were sunk to the old Black Vein Seam.

Risca Colliery, which was originally owned by the London and South Wales Colliery Company.

In Loving Memory

of the
3508 MINERS WHO LOST THEIR LIVES
COLLIERY DISASTERS
IN NORTH WALES, SOUTH WALES, AND MONMOUTHSHIRE
DURING THE PAST 90 YEARS.

Date & Place	Killed.
1837—May 10, Plas-yr-Argoed, Mold	21
1837—June 17, Blaina (Mon.)	21
1844—January 1, Dinas	12
1845—August 2, Cwmbach	28
1846—January 14, Risca	35
1848—June 21, Victoria (Mon.)	11
1849—Aug. 11, Letty Shenkin, Aberdare	52
1850—Dec. 14, New Duffryn Colliery	13
1852—May 10, Duffryn	64
1853—March 12, Risca Vale	10
1856—July 13, Cymmer	114
1858—October 13, Duffryn	20
1859—April 5, Neath, Chain Colliery	26
1860—December 1, Risca	146
1862—February 19, Gethin, Merthyr	47
1863—October 17, Morgam	39
1863—December 24, Maesteg	14
1865—June 16, Tredegar	2
1865—December 20, Upper Gethin	30
1867—November 8, Ferndale	178
1869—May 23, Llanerch	7
1869—June 10, Ferndale	60
1870—July 23, Llansamlet	19
1871—February 24, Pentre	38
1871—October 4, Gelli Pit, Aberdare	4
1872—Jan. 10, Oakwood, Llynvi Valley.	11
1872—March 2, Victoria	19
1872—March 8, Wernfach	18
1874—April 5, Abertillery	6
1874—July 24, Charles Pit, Llansamlet.	19
1875—December 4, New Tredegar	22
1875—December 6, Llan Pit, Pentyrch	12
1876—December 13, Abertillery	20
1877—March 8, Worcester Pit, Swansea.	18
1878—September 1, Abercarn	62
1878—September 11, Abercarn	268
1879—January 13, Dinas	3
1879—Sept. 22, Waunllwyd, Ebbw Vale.	84
1880—July 15, Risca	119
1880—Dec. 10, Naval Steam Colliery	96
1882—January 15, Risca	4
1882—February 11, Coedcae	6
1883—February 1, Coedcae	5
1883—August 21, Gelli	4
1884—January 16, Cwmavon	10
1884—January 23, Penygraig	11
1884—Nov 8, Pochin Colliery, Tredegar.	14
1886—Naval Colliery	14
1885—December 24, Mardy	81
1887—February 18, Ynyshir	37
1888—May 14, Aber, Tynewydd	5
1890—January 20, Glrn Pit, Pontypool.	5
1890—February 6, Llanerch	176
1890—March 8, Morfa	87
1892—August 12, Great Western Colliery	58
1892—August 26, Park Slip	110
1894—June 25, Cilfynydd	276
1896—January 28, Tylorstown	57
1899—August 18, Llest Colliery, Garw.	19
1901—May 24, Sengenhydd	82
1901—September 10, Llanbradach	12
1905—March 10, Clydach Vale	31
1905—July 5, Wattstown	119
1913—October 13, Senghenydd	436
1923—April 26, Trimsaran	9
1927—March 1, Cwm, Ebbw Vale	52

A sudden change; at God's command they fell:
They had no chance to bid their friends farewell;
Swift came the blast, without a warning given,
And bid them haste to meet their God in Heaven.

Memorial to the 3508 Miners who lost their lives 1837 to 1927.

102

CHAPTER FIVE

By the begining of the twentieth century, the mining community of the Sirhowy Valley had found its feet. It was a complete population, rather than a group of strangers who had moved in from other parts of Wales and from England, to make a living in the pits.

Two or three new generations had grown up in the Valley, developing their own culture and their own homeland. Despite the many difficulties faced by all the inhabitants, there was a feeling of friendship and kinship in the communities, based on the sharing of hardship and a feeling of unity that had never existed before.

The role of women in the mining communities had changed, although some of them still worked on the pit surfaces, screening coal and performing other arduous manual tasks, they no longer worked underground. Single girls who did not want to do this kind of work traditionally went into service, if no suitable post was available near home, they moved away to the houses of those who could afford servants. Married women were expected to stay at home, to keep house for their husbands and usually, their large families.

'Mam', as she was usually called in the Welsh Valleys, was very houseproud, keeping her home scrupulously clean despite all the dirt and dust that was brought into it from the grimy clothes and bodies of her husband and sons when they returned from the pit. Before the days of pithead baths, she would have to heat the water on the stove for the men to take a bath in the traditional tin tub in front of the fire. Cleaning, cooking, washing and caring for her family occupied Mam's full hard day.

Despite all the booms, depressions, and strikes of earlier years, there was more stability among the communities in the Valley than there had been before, but it was not without cost. Throughout the Welsh coalfield, between 1837 and 1927 a total of 3,508 miners had lost their lives in colliery disasters. Some who died in the Sirhowy Valley are recorded here:

		Number Killed
1846	Risca	35
1853	Risca Vale	10
1860	Risca	146
1865	Bedwellty	25
1865	Tredegar	2
1872	Lower Plas, Blackwood	5
1880	Black Vein	120
1882	Risca	4
1884	Pochin	14

These are some of the recorded disasters, others which may have occurred in small workings were not always recorded. The statistics do not show the numbers of miners who died as a result of earlier injury in the pit, or from lung disease and infection due to poor working conditions, deprivation or poverty.

The industrial revolution had swept like a forest fire through the whole of South Wales, and the people who survived it were stronger, more assertive people who had become aware of their collective power and their ability to order their own lives. This attitude, which had developed slowly over the previous century, was fostered by the Miners' Unions which developed from the earlier Friendly Societies.

Up to the 1890s, when the Miners' Federation of Great Britain was formed, only 45,000 out of 120,000 miners across the South Wales Coalfield belonged to a Union. 1898, however, saw a turning point when the South Wales Miners Federation was set up to cover the whole coalfield. By 1899 it had 104,000 members and had become the strongest Union area in the country.

The influence of the coal mining industry on the community was far greater than the effects of the usual worker/employer relationship. The miners had become a brotherhood, linked by danger and hardship and by their Union. For the first time, they tasted political power, their leader William Abraham (Mabon) had been elected to Parliament for the new Rhondda seat in 1885, and in 1900 Keir Hardie was elected to Parliment for Merthyr Tydfil, the first Labour M.P. for Wales.

The miners were building Miners' Institutes, with libraries, reading rooms and facilities for meetings and social occasions. There was increased concern for the well being of the community, for its health and education and in the Sirhowy Valley this manifested itself as early as 1871 when the Tredegar Health and Education Fund was formed by the workers employed by the Tredegar Iron and Coal Company. The members were all employed in either the ironworks or the collieries in Tredegar.

The initial contribution was threepence in the pound on all earnings, and for this the members were entitled to relief if they fell sick or were unable to work because of an accident. The fund also helped to maintain some schools in the area.

In 1890 the Society became known as the Tredegar Workman's Medical Aid and Sick Relief Fund and there were nearly 5,000 members. The threepence in the pound contribution was maintained, twopence of which was used to pay for medical staff, and the purchase of medicines and appliances. The remaining money was put into the fund for sick relief. Other members, not employed by the Tredegar Iron and Coal Company were able to join, and obtained all the benefits except sick pay.

By 1900, the society employed four doctors and a dentist and embarked on building the Tredegar General Hospital, which opened in 1904. In addition, they had two surgeries and an office in the town, and the Society also owned the Doctors' houses. This, now substantial organisation, was held to be far in advance in terms of benefit to its members, than any similar Society. In 1913 it became the Tredegar Workmans' Medical Aid Society.

One of the Doctors employed by the Society, from 1922 to 1924, was Dr. A.J. Cronin, who lived in one of the Society's houses with his wife who assisted in the Society's dispensary. A.J. Cronin's book, 'The Citadel' was based on his experiences in Tredegar.

Aneurin Bevan, who had been a miner at Ty Trist and later at Pochin, became a Committee Member of the Society, before he became an M.P. He later became Minister of Health in the Labour

The Right Hon. Aneurin Bevan became a M.P. in 1929 after being a miner in Ty Trist and Pochin Collieries. He was Minster of Health in the post-war Labour Government and pioneered the National Health Service. The Tredegar Miners Medical Aid Society had provided such a service in micro-cosm from 1890. The photograph shows him at a Tredegar Carnival in the late 1940s.

On land at the top of Sirhowy Hill are these monumental stones placed to honour the life of revered Labour Member of Parliament for the district Aneurin 'Nye' Bevan.

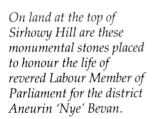

The late Mr. David Norris, in the 1970s, shovels in his delivery of coal at his home in Glyn Terrace Tredegar.

Government and was instrumental in developing the National Health Service, which he said was based on the Tredegar Workmans' Aid Society. The contributions to the National Health Service far exceeded those paid by the Tredegar Workmen to their Society, which in 1948 was threepence per week. The contribution covered all their dependants and included medical treatment, expenses to hospital, provision of spectacles, dentures and artificial limbs and a vast range of other medical provision. It also included benefits to retired members and their widows.

Mrs. Norah Childs, Secretary to the to the Society from 1941 to 1995 writes:

'The people of Tredegar are worse off today. What we enjoyed before 1948, the majority of Britain have today, but they are paying more for facilities than we did. It is 45 years since the National Health Service came in and we are still paying our way.' (1993)

The Society was dissolved on 31 December 1994. Membership at that date was 81 paying members, 144 retired members, and 187 widows.

1913 was the year of peak production in the South Wales Coalfield, when the production figure reached a zenith of almost 57 million tons. Due to the number of miners who were called to serve in the 1914-1918 war, production was reduced at the crucial time when demand from the Admiralty was very high. The coalworkers pressed a demand for higher wages in 1915 in response to the demands on them to increase productivity. The colliers' demands, which resulted in a strike, brought them into greater opposition than ever, not only with coal owners, but with the Government. A Royal Commission was set up to investigate the situation, and in 1919 the Report supported the miners' unions recommendation that the coal industry should be nationalised.

The dispute was now between the three groups most involved in the coal industry, the coal owners, the miners, and the Government. The general unrest resulted in a decline in production between 1921 and 1936 and the number of working miners was almost halved. In addition, there were a series of strikes during the period including the General Strike and Miners Lock Out in 1926, when miners who had refused to accept the Coalowners terms for a cut in pay and an extra hour on their working day, were locked out of work.

This period of national depression, when there were thousands of miners and other workers unemployed throughout the Valleys, led to a time of emigration for many Valley communities. People travelled far into more prosperous areas of the United Kingdom and abroad to find work. Those who stayed at home, had a struggle to survive on unemployment benefit which was about 20 shillings (£1) a week for a man and his family of four.

During the Second World War 1939 to 1945 the coal industry was taken over by the Government. When the War finished the newly elected Labour Government, which included former South Wales Miners' Leaders such as Aneurin Bevan and James Griffiths, nationalised the mines. The National Coal Board, when it came into being in 1947, nationalised the remaining collieries still working in the Sirhowy Valley.

South Wales Marchers' Organising Council.

SOUTH WALES MINERS'
MARCH TO LONDON

CALL TO ACTION!   VOLUNTEERS WANTED!

Arising out of the pronouncement by A. J. COOK, 18/9/27, a Miners' March to London from S. Wales is being organised. The March will commence on the day Parliament opens--Nov. 8th, and the Marchers will arrive in London on Nov. 20th, where they will be received by an All London Working Class Demonstration.

The object of the March shall be two-fold, to arouse a Nation-wide feeling concerning the Appalling Conditions in the Mine-fields created by the policy of the Government and the Coal-owners, and to seek an interview with the Prime Minister, the Minister of Mines, the Minister of Labour, and the Minister of Health.

A notice calling miners to the 'Miners March' (also known as the 'Hunger March') in 1927, which was during a period of national economic depression and mass unemployment.

Dates shown are opening and closing dates of the nationalised collieries listed north to south along the Valley.

Colliery	Opening		Closing
Ty Trist Colliery	1834	to	1959
Pochin Colliery	1880	to	1965
Rock Colliery	1900	to	1957
Markham Navigation Colliery	1912	to	1985
Waterloo Colliery	1908	to	1970
Oakdale Navigation Colliery	1908	to	1989
Wyllie Colliery	1926	to	1968
Nine Mile Point Colliery	1902	to	1964
Risca Colliery	1878	to	1967

Despite nationalisation, which was welcomed in the South Wales Coalfield, production continued to decline as seams became worked out and pits were closed. The National Coal Board (later to be British Coal) was unwilling to keep what they referred to as 'uneconomic pits' open. Gradually, all were closed in the South Wales Valleys, and the closure of Oakdale Navigation Colliery in 1989, meant there are no more coal mines in the Sirhowy Valley, or indeed in Gwent.

The colliers of the Valley did not simply create wealth for the coal owners and the major industries. Whilst they earned their living, their industry created the towns and villages which are now inhabited by their descendants.

Newport overtook Swansea in 1823 as the main coal exporting port and in the 1830s became the largest in the country. It was superseded by Cardiff in the 1840s when the Rhondda Valleys were in major production of coal.

Newport's thriving port which exported about five and a half millions tons of coal from the Gwent Valleys in the peak year of 1914, became the important town it is today largely as a result of the success of the collieries. Tredegar House, the home of the Morgans of Tredegar, now owned by Newport Borough Council, shows evidence of the wealth accrued by Lord Morgan who owned the 'Golden Mile' along which the coal trains ran to the docks.

It took 300 million years for the tree - like plants of the primeval forest that grew on the steep slopes above the Sirhowy River to turn into coal. Squeezed by the constant pressure of rock, changing, decaying, evolving from living matter to organic fossil, the resulting 'black gold' influenced the lives of thousands of people.

It took 300 million years to form coal, and a little more than 200 years to rip it out. Against that scale of unimaginable time, 200 years is just one moment. Some would say it was a terrible moment, wasteful of lives and precious, unrenewable resources. Others, looking from a different perspective would see a glorious, heroic moment. Whatever our view, it cannot be ignored or forgotten.

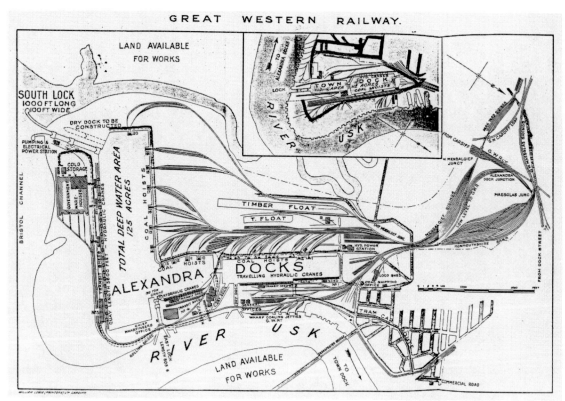

A plan of Newport Docks, 1924.

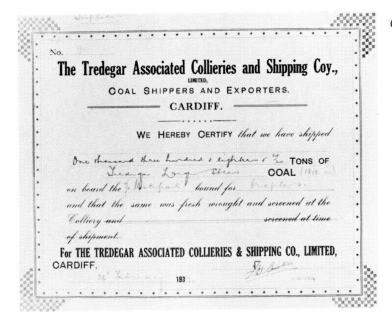

The Tredegar Associated Collieries and Shipping Coy.,
LIMITED,

COAL SHIPPERS AND EXPORTERS.

CARDIFF.

WE HEREBY CERTIFY *that we have shipped*

One thousand three hundred & eighteen & ¹⁸/₂₀ TONS OF

Tredegar Large Steam COAL *(1318 tons)*

on board the S.S. Uskport bound for Naples

and that the same was fresh wrought and screened at the

Colliery and ~~screened at time~~

of shipment.

For THE TREDEGAR ASSOCIATED COLLIERIES & SHIPPING CO., LIMITED,
CARDIFF.

193

Certificate of Shipping of 1,318 tons of large steam coal from Tredegar on board the S.S. Uskport bound for Naples in 1937.

Pit props at Newport Docks awaiting despatch to the collieries.

111

Valley coal being loaded on board ship at Newport Docks during the 1920s.

Export of Coal and Coke at South Wales Ports

Year	Cardiff	Penarth	Barry	Newport	Port Talbot	Swansea	Llanelli
1885	6,678,133	2,795,025	-	2,684,111	-	1,239,338	-
1895	7,542,220	2,507,913	5,051,822	3,359,829	-	1,721,079	-
1905	7,294,020	3,740,061	8,651,511	4,186,430	1,072,676	2,653,447	376,565
1914	10,278,963	3,992,405	10,875,510	5,465,713	1,711,808	3,749,449	288,762

Vessel loading coal for export at Newport Docks circa 1920s.

Some fifty years later and the mining of Welsh Valley coal has come to a sad end. The result is to be witnessed in the photograph where a vessel is seen discharging imported coal at Newport c.1970.

Shown by location, irrespective of local authority boundaries. Dates shown are the approximate dates of operation, if known. Names of owning companies shown in order of succession of ownership. Although extensive, this may not be a comprehensive list, many small workings being unrecorded.

ARGOED

Abernant Colliery. Markham 1880-1932. Linked underground with Llanover Colliery. Bargoed Coal Co.

Argoed Colliery. 1888. Morgan and Sons/E.D.Williams/Budd and Co.

Cwrt-y-Bella Level. c 1820. Thomas Prothero.

Cwm Crych Colliery. Closed c 1900.

Darren Felyn.

Farmers Level.

Golynos. Early 19th century.

Gwrhay. 1809. Moses Moses.

Hafodyrisclawdd. 1816. Sir Henry Protheroe.

Hollybush Old and New Collieries, includes Darren and Pontygwaith 1888-1921 E.D.Williams/ (and others later).

Islwyn Colliery, Argoed. 1917-1948. William Barnes Mimes/E.H.Bennet.

Llanover Colliery. Mile south of Markham. Bargoed Coal Co. Taken over by Tredegar Iron and Coal Co. in 1929 as a pumping station to protect Oakdale Colliery.

Manmoel Levels (3). 1816-1925, Manmoel Colliery Co./C.Pond.

Markham Navigation Colliery. 1912-1985. Markham Coal Co. (subsidiary of Tredegar Iron and Coal Company). Explosion April 1912 killed 6 men. Linked to Oakdale Navigation Colliery in World War 2 as a way out if bombed, also in 1979 when output was diverted to Oakdale.

Penderi Level. c 1814. Llewellyn Llewellyn.

Rhoswen. early 19th century. Adjacent to Golynos.

Twyn Simon Level. Closed 1930s. Bowditch Brothers.

Westfield.

BLACKWOOD

Cwm Gelli (Gelli Levels). 1878. D.Thomas/Budd and Co./Bowditch and Sons.

Cwm Philkins Colliery.

Chapel Colliery. (Near Libanus Chapel).

Factory.

Gelli Dwylt. 1850-1900. D.Lewis.

Glyngaer Colliery. 1870s E.D.Williams.

Lewis.

Libanus. with Chapel Colliery. 1880-1922. Bevan and Pryce/Edmund Mathews.

Lower Libanus. With Chapel Colliery.

Maes-y-Ryddid Level. early 1900s.

Mount Pleasant.

Penmaen Old and New.

Penrhiw and Woodfieldside Collieries. 1815-1924. Evan and Lewis Lewis/W.Baker/Penrhiw and
Woodfieldside Colliery Co./B.P.Harris/Woodfield Collieries Ltd./Penmaen Colliery Co.

Penwaingoch Colliery. 1870s. E.Williams.

Plas Bedwellty Colliery. (also known as Lower Plas) 19th century. Now Bus Station site.

Primrose Colliery. Mid 19th century. Closed 1946. C.Pond./Walter Bevan.

Pwlldu.

Rock Colliery, early 19th century - 1957, Rock Coal Co./Budd and Co./National Coal Board.
Includes Rock Pit. New Rock. Rock Levels.

Upper Gellideg Colliery. 1840s.

CROSSKEYS

Bensons.

Drill Hall.

Jack-y-North.

Rock Vein.

Waunfawr.

Old Black Vein Colliery. 120 men were killed in 1880.

CWMFELINFACH

Nine Mile Point (formerly Coronation) Colliery.
1902-1964. Burnyeat and Brown/Ocean Coal. Co/Ocean and United Coal. Co./National Coal
Board.
In 1905 during sinking a landslide killed seven men.
In 1935 there was a stay-down strike for 128 and 177 hours against the use of 'scab labour' from the
South Wales Industrial Union.

FLEUR-DE-LYS

Gelli-Haf. 1850-1900 (two levels) H.F. Jones and Harris and Co.

Gelli Haf Issaf. late 19th century. W. Moor and Co.
Upper Buttery Hatch Colliery. 1840s.

MYNYDDISLWYN

Beddoes.
Caerllwyn.
Church Land. c.1820.
Darren Ddu.
Dyffryn.
Islwyn.
Pantyresk c.1830.
Tirbach.
Twyn Gwyn.
Tyr y Berth Colliery. 1870s D.Jones.

OAKDALE

Martins Level. 19th century.
Oakdale Navigation Colliery. 1908-1989. (last deep colliery in Gwent).Produced 1 million tons in 1930, manpower then 2,000. Largest colliery in South Wales by 1986. Linked to Markham 1979, and Celynon North 1981. Oakdale Navigation Co. (subsidiary of Tredegar Iron and Coal Co)/ National Coal Board.
Waterloo Colliery. 1908-1970. House coal Pit. Oakdale Navigation Co (see above) National Coal Board. Became Training Centre for mines.
Waterloo Level. (named after the battle) 1815-1920s. Davis and Morgan/W.Griffiths and Co./ Waterloo Colliery Co.
Woodfield Levels. Late 19th century.

PENTWYNMAWR

Kingcoed (CinCoed) 1921. Bush Colliery Co.
Pennar.
Pennar Ganol.
Pennar Junction.
Penmynydd.
Pontymista.
Ton-y-Moch.
Ton-y-Pistill.
Tynllwyn Level. Early 19th century.

PONTLLANFRAITH

Berris.
Bryn. c.1820-1850. now site of Bryn Junior School.
Butts.
Cwm Philkins. or Llys Pentwyn. 19th century.
Diamond Colliery. opposite Pioneer.
Factory Gelligroes Collieries. (2) 1804-1887. Gelligroes Colliery Co.
Islwyn Colliery. Many levels. 1888. E. Thomas.
Mynyddislwyn Colliery.
New Tir Philkins Colliery. late 19th century.
Penllwyn. c.1805. Joseph Beaumont.
Penmaen.
Tir Philkins Drift. 1880. E. Beddoe. Pioneer Site.
Tycopi Colliery. 1870. Evan Morgan.
Ty Llwyd Colliery. Rees Bros. 1878-1888.
Woodfield. early 19th century. Islwyn Transport Depot.
Wyllie Colliery 1926-1968. Tredegar (Southern) Collieries Ltd. (subsidiary of Tredegar Iron Coal Co./National Coal Board.

TREDEGAR

About 80 known coal workings of which a few are listed.

Bedwellty Pits. 1800s-1940s. Tredegar Iron and Coal Co. 16 June 1865 26 men killed in explosion.
Gamster Colliery, Sirhowy. 1913 D. Morris.
Glanhowy Colliery, Sirhowy. 1920s D.G. Jenkins and Co.
Graham's Navigation Colliery (also known as No.9 or Sirhowy Colliery). 1840-1913. Grahams Navigation (Merthyr) Co., Ltd.
Graham's Navigation Levels (see above).
Plantation Colliery. 1920s D.Williams and Son.
Pochin Colliery. 1880-1965. Tredegar Iron and Coal Co./National Coal Board. Near site of old furnace at Pontygwaith-yr-Haian.
Tredegar Pits. All small pits owned by Tredegar Iron Co. none of which worked in 20th century.

1.	Bryn Bach. 1818.		7.	Mountain. 1841.	
2.	Evan Davies. 1821.		8.	Steven Charles. 1838.	
3.	Quick. 1834.		9.	1839.	
4.	Briggs. 1830.		10.	Yard. 1838.	
5.	Globe. 1840.		11.	Evan Evans 1839-1897.	
6.	Doctors. 1832.		12.	David Jervis 1840-1897.	

BIBLIOGRAPHY

Evan Powell	History of Tredegar
Oliver Jones	The Early Days of Sirhowy and Tredegar
W. Scandrett	Old Tredegar
Harry Lewis	Gwent Panorama
David Egan	South Wales Mining Valleys
Ralph Thomas	Oakdale the Model Village
Michael Eyres	Masters of the Coalfield
W.W. Tasker	Railways in the Sirhowy Valley
Ray Lawrence	Directory of the Coal Workings of the South Wales Coalfield
Ness Edwards	The Industrial Revolution in South Wales
Harold Finch	Memoirs of a Bedwellty M.P.
Aubrey Boyles	The History of the Monmouthshire Railway and Canal Company

Various documents from the archives of:

Gwent County Council
National Museum of Wales
South Wales Miners' Library
Reference libraries throughout Gwent
Monmouthshire Merlin, South Wales Argus, Western Mail, South Wales Echo
Newspaper Reports
Islwyn Borough Council Guides and Notes
Tredegar Town Clerk Tredegar Town Guides
Mrs. Norah Childs Notes about the Tredegar Medical Aid Society